68

John Kim, MA, MFT

John Kim

ISBN:1475212674
ISBN-13:1475212674

I believe the greatest problem with men today is that there is a lack of them.

We live in a fatherless nation. Most of our fathers were / are physically or emotionally absent. I have seen the effects of this in the men and women I coach daily as well as the kids I have treated in residential for substance abuse. The absent father contributes to eating disorders, addictions, dysfunctional / abusive relationships, co-dependency, low self esteem, depression, and suicide.

I believe most men are not aware of their impact. They are oblivious to the emotional destruction they leave behind. I believe this is partly due to not having a positive male role model while growing up. This cycle needs to be broken. I believe now more than ever, men have a responsibility to take ownership and redefine themselves. And women must raise the bar and set a standard for the kind of men they want in their lives.

ACKNOWLEDGMENTS

I want to thank all the men out there who have decided to look at themselves with courage to change, all the men making an honest effort to be good fathers, better husbands, and kinder friends, men who have sacrificed for their family, neighbors, and country. I want to thank men working in mental health, hospitals, and classrooms, men who wear uniforms, police officers, fire fighters, and soldiers. These are the true leaders of our world and I hope to follow in your footsteps.

We are not born men. We are born boys. Although we may take the shape of one on the exterior, the transition into manhood is an internal process. One that requires much work - reflection, pain, courage, and sometimes a rebirth. It is a process that never ends. There is no completion. Being a man is not a state. It is a journey. Many choose to embark on this journey. Many do not.

The following is a collection of behavioral traits, dos and don't, that I believe define a man. I believe they contribute to a healthier relationship in all forms, especially with self. This accumulation is based on my experiences as a friend, son, brother, boyfriend, husband, and therapist. I do not claim to posses all of these traits. I actually struggle with most of them. You may or may not agree with them. Some are light. Some are heavy. They are in no particular order.

My intent in writing this book is to create a dialogue. Nothing else. My hope is that if you are a man, it encourages you to think about who you want to be. If you are a woman, who you want to be with.

Enjoy.

#1 Don't React. Do Respond.

We react from pain. Someone insulted us, broke our heart, or didn't truly listen. This hurt encourages us to behave without a filter. It's our way of protecting ourselves. Or so we think. Reacting is actually self disruptive behavior. When we react, we are not creating a space to heal. Instead, we are passing on our pain. The results are arguments that quickly turn into wild fires, characters assassinated, and failed relationships. When we react, we are picking scabs, usually our own.

On the other hand, a response requires thought, patience, and a plan. A response means thinking of the best way to speak / behave in a given situation that will serve to heal instead of destroy. This requires work. It means practicing metacognition and empathy, biting your tongue and or swallowing your ego. The results are resolved conflict, increased trust, and strengthened relationships. When we respond, we are applying ointment.

MEN: Reacting is to take. Responding is to give. Reacting is about you. Responding is about "us". Boys react. Men respond.

WOMEN: The key word here is control. If your man reacts instead of responds, he is not in control of his emotions / behavior and this emotional instability will manifest into the relationship. It will eventually come in the form of abuse, emotional and or physical.

2 Don't Pee in the Shower

They know.

MEN: It doesn't matter how much shampoo you flush it down with, women have a stronger sense of smell than you do. Just because you can't detect it, it doesn't mean they can't. But this is not about odor. It's about trust, assuming your wife / girlfriend does not approve of this behavior and has expressed that to you. If she's cool with it, read no further. It's fair game. Write your name on the wall. But if she disapproves and you're aware of that, the act of doing something behind her back is what this is really about. Behavior bleeds. If you're doing this, you may also be feeding the dog under the table, listening to your iPod on your motorcycle, or flirting with the babysitter. Peeing in the shower is one of those "what else" behaviors. If he's doing this, what else is he doing? It opens a can of worms, creates hairline cracks in trust. Enough of these cracks and suddenly she doesn't want to go down on you anymore. Trust me. It's not worth it. Hold it until you get out.

WOMEN: We like to pee on things. We did it as kids. We do it as adults. If you don't want us to do it, you have to tell us. Don't assume. That's not fair. Peeing in the shower isn't an obvious "no" like leaving the toilet seat up. Some women don't mind. They even do it themselves although they will probably never admit it. So let him know exactly how you feel about him marking his territory in a place where you don't wear shores. Use it as an exercise to build trust and communication instead of another reason to seek couples counseling.

#3 Do Walk with Mirrors

Walking with mirrors means shattering the version of you that is false. In order to know which version that is, we must examine our thoughts, behavior, and the affect we have on others. It means to be metacognitive, having the ability to think about your thoughts. Also, to take responsibility for them which means to explore wiring and making a motion to rewire. This process is on going. To walk with mirrors means to constantly examine self and to seek growth and truth.

MEN: Think about all the men you admire, from professional athletes to CEOs to musicians to your favorite grandfather. Who do you admire the most and why? You may be in awe of a man's ability. The way Donald Trump makes money, Tiger woods sinks balls, and Tony Robbins motivates millions. But the person you will admire the most will be the one who admits his defects and does something about it. He will be the man who is vulnerable, transparent, and non-defensive. He will be humble and honest. He will not be the man with the greatest ability. He will be the man with the most character.

WOMEN: Any man can build abs. Any man can make money. Find a man who walks with mirrors and you will not only find a man, you will find a leader, a hero.

#4 Do Make Your Bed

MEN: Why fix something that's just going to get messed up ten hours later? Besides, who's gonna see it? Right? Also, that ten extra minutes can go toward an apple fritter on the way to work. Or maybe you feel like it's not your job to make the bed. You're in charge of changing the oil and mowing the lawn. But here's the truth. Your relationship is at stake. On the surface, making your bed shows that you are clean, responsible, and willing to contribute to the household chores. But on a deeper level, the subconscious, you are announcing to your partner, but more importantly to yourself that you are going somewhere. You are now leaving to conquer the world. You have direction, a dream in your head, a fire in your belly. It is a rite of passage for the modern man. He is certain, fearless, and determined.

I know you're rolling your eyes but humor me for a moment. Women desire a man with direction. Without it, she will begin to doubt you, and a woman in doubt is a relationship in trouble. The chemistry will change. Her attraction toward you will dissolve and she won't know why. She will blame it on surface things like your dirty socks and why you "need" HBO. Making your bed isn't about making your bed. It's about the subtext, the subconscious message / energy you are sending out. You are saying you have direction. You are saying you're going to go out and conquer the world. So make your bed or the only thing you'll be doing on it is sleeping.

WOMEN: You don't want him to make the bed. You want him to want to make the bed. I get it. How do you do this? Support him in his endeavors and make him feel invincible. Let him know that what he gets up to do every single morning is important and that you are proud of him. Be consistent and mean it. Then one day, you will scramble out of the bathroom, late for work again, to find the sheets perfectly tucked, pillows fluffed, and little note that says "I appreciate you".

#5 Do Be Gay Friendly

Our upbringing contributes to our programing. That is a fact and a factor but not an excuse. As we maneuver through the world, we challenge what was fed to us and form our own beliefs. That being said, we have the right to believe whatever we want. But there is a difference between belief and behavior. One affects others.

This isn't about sexual orientation. It's about judgement and control. When we act differently toward someone based on anything other than their character / heart, we are placing judgment on them. We are reacting to the fact that they don't fall into our shoulds and should nots. This resistance stems from control or lack there of. When things don't fit into our mold, we panic, squirm, and try to change. Or we blame, judge, and run. Growth means getting comfortable with the uncomfortable. If you feel yourself judging someone based on their sexual orientation, I encourage you to see it as an opportunity for growth.

MEN: Just because someone is gay doesn't mean he is wants to have sex with you. Read that sentence again. I think a lot of men are uncomfortable around gay men because they feel like the gay men are attracted to them. You don't assume a woman is attracted to you just because you are heterosexual, do you? You may wish this but we both know it's not the case. Okay, so maybe it's not in your head. Maybe the gay guy is attracted to you. Wouldn't the fact that another human finds you attractive be a compliment?

WOMEN: It's obvious that homophobia is a direct reflection on one's own security. But my concern has less to do with what he thinks of himself and more to do with how he treats you. If someone judges and controls in one area of his life, chances are he will in others.

6 Don't Argue

Arguments are usually about two hurt people not being heard. But instead of hearing each other and addressing the hurt, we get into a rat race to see who can pull out the most shit from the past.

MEN: Break the cycle. She's arguing with you because she's not feeling heard. So put your point aside and focus on making her feel heard. You do this by practicing empathy, putting yourself in her shoes. Try to truly understand what she's going through. This means address her feelings. Once she feels heard, the argument can now turn into a discussion. Express your point. If it gets heated again, don't argue. Go back to addressing her feelings, making her feel heard. Make it a non-negotiable that you will not argue. It takes two people to have a tug of war. If you refuse to hold the rope, there is no war.

Well why should I back down first?

What do you get from being right other than resentment and a stiff back from sleeping on the couch?

I can't believe I'm doing this but I'm going to quote Dr. Phil.
"Do you want to be right or do you want to be happy?"

WOMEN: Exactly the same thing I said to the men.

#7 Don't Compare Yourself to Other Men (Yes, I'm talking about penis size)

At around age nine, we discover our penis and become fascinated by it. Although it's always been there, we are suddenly intrigued and curious. We can't take it apart so we start playing with it. We realize it gives us pleasure, a new sensation. It makes us feel powerful. Subconsciously, we begin to associate penis with power. This cognition is what will drive us to purchase Hummers and over sized homes later in life.

The requirement to change for gym class in middle school alerts us that wands come in different sizes. Our power is now compared with others. We go from feeling like Superman to Clark Kent. Now we're taking an object and internalizing it to determine our worth. This thought pattern brings us anxiety and makes us feel less than. It is a pattern we will struggle with as we go through life.

Then we discover porn. Now we're not even Clark Kent. We're the intern at the Daily Planet pushing mail carts and dodging staplers. Since changing our size is not an option, we try to make up for it in other ways, in a classroom, at work, and on the court. Or in objects, cars, houses, company bonuses, and women

(Not calling women objects. Referring to them as an external perception of measurement).

Soon we're comparing everything we have with other men and we become workaholics, alcoholics, and can't get it up anymore from all the stress and anxiety. We lose the very thing that once made us feel powerful.

MEN: There is no magic in your wand. Your power lies in a different organ, your heart. And if a woman is not satisfied with your size, you are with the wrong woman.

WOMEN: Understand that a man comparing / competing with other men is ingrained and started way before he met you. If you belittle a man's penis in bed, even as a joke, or say anything to indicate that you think it's small, what he is hearing is that he's powerless. So instead of focusing on his size, focus on his ability. Give him a cape, not a complex.

#8 Do Drive with Courtesy

My best friend egged me on in the next lane. That's why I did it. Within five seconds, I surpassed the freeway speed limit in my brand new Mazda RX-7 twin turbo. I think I was going 95mph when my girlfriend screamed "stop!" But I ignored her. I had something to prove. I wanted to win. Looking back, I don't remember who won the race. All I remember is the terror etched in my girlfriend's face as tears streamed down her pale cheeks.

The doctor who recently examined my chest nearly broke every bone in her body when her driver fell asleep at the wheel and swerved off the side of the road. She was traveling with a group of friends. She was the only survivor. My ex-wife's best friend has permanent brain damage because a drunk driver swerved into her lane. My girlfriend lost five friends to automobile accidents. I can go on and on but I don't need to. You have your own stories of how innocent lives have been taken because of boys like me.

MEN: I understand you like driving fast. I get the adrenaline rush. But once you get into your vehicle, whether you have a passenger or not, you are putting lives at stake. This means you have a responsibility. Well what's the point of having a performance car if I'm not going to drive it fast? I feel the exact same way. The answer is take it to the track.

WOMEN: If your man refuses to drive safely with you in the car, imagine what he's driving like when you're not in the car. You can't do anything about his actions when he's alone but if he doesn't drive with caution while you're in the vehicle after you have asked him to, that is called emotional abuse. Period. Get out of the car. Maybe even the relationship.

9 Do Have a Firm Handshake

There are two types of men. Men who look you in the eye and shake your hand firmly and men who look down at their shoes and hand you a dead fish. The first is the type of man who makes decisions. He is confident. He knows who he is. You can trust him. He is honorable. The second is filled with ambivalence. He's indecisive and unsure of himself. He is slippery and avoidant. He doesn't handle confrontation well. He cuts corners when possible, doesn't know where to go on dates, is selfish in bed and runs funny. All this from a handshake? Yes. A man's handshake says everything about him.

Our handshake reflects our perception of self. A weak grip and scrambling eyes stem from ambivalence and insecurity. We believe we are not enough, less than. This false belief causes us to look for short cuts and avoid confrontations. It's a way of hiding. We are afraid. On the other hand, a firm handshake stems from certainty, a belief that we are enough. A strong grip with eye contact and a confident smile says I am valuable, I am worthy, and I am here. A pleasure to meet you.

MEN: The next time you shake someone's hand, grip it with authority. Remind yourself what the behavior means, the message it sends to the other person but more importantly to yourself. You matter. You exist. You affect others. Even if you doubt yourself, make sure your handshake doesn't say that. By changing behavior, beliefs can also change. See it as an opportunity for growth. Introduce yourself to the world.

WOMEN: If any man gives you a dead fish for a handshake, don't accept it. Tell him you would like a real one. Show him if he doesn't understand. If you're going to take the time to meet someone, meet someone. Make sure he presents himself to you appropriately. You don't deserve luke warm.

#10 Don't Be a Double Douche

Every man was or will be a douche at one point in his life. When we're scoring touchdowns in high school, receiving letters on our chest in college, landing that corner office in our twenties. There's no way around it. It's like puberty. All men go through it. But the key is to not do it twice. We only get one free get out of being a douche card.

What is a douche? Any posturing behavior that stems from insecurity or ego. Examples of being a douche include but are not limited to, purchasing a bright yellow Ferrari because you can, not because you're a car enthusiast. Yelling obscenities at the elderly. Checking yourself in every reflection. Tattoos purely for aesthetics. Crunchy hair. Not controlling your alcohol. Grabbing women. Starting fights with men. Bicep curls. Fake bake. Teeth that glow in the dark. Sporting sunglasses indoors. Controlling your girlfriend. Being the loudest voice in the room. Flavored condoms. Animal cruelty. Pulling in front of the car that cut you off and slamming your brakes. Not tipping. Tossing your keys at the valet guy instead of handing them to him. Way too much cologne. Demanding to speak with the manager in restaurants. V-necks that meet at your belly button. Refusing to turn down your car stereo while people are trying to have a conversation. Being creepy. Motorcycles that set off car alarms. Bullying. Cursing and graphic sexual language in front of women. Over tipping to impress others.

MEN: Although it may feel empowering, this behavior only announces your insecurity.

WOMEN: If you're not attracted to these guys, why do you keep dating them?

#11 Do Put Thought into Your Gifts

The invention of the gift card. Although brilliantly obvious, it's cheating. It's like reading the Cliff Notes instead of the entire book. Just by picking the store you want her to shop at doesn't turn cash into a thoughtful gift. It's not a gift. It's an easy way out. Or in.

Think about all the gifts you've received in the last five years. Of the ones you can actually match faces to, which were the most memorable and why? What's the common thread? Assuming you didn't wake up on your birthday to a helicopter on your front lawn, most likely it was the thought, the effort, and a piece of the giver - the giver has put his or her essence into the gift. The greatest gifts always contain a part of the gifter. That is why it's memorable, unique, and one of a kind. The "holy shit" factor of a helicopter may be memorable. But a poem from your six year old daughter, a painting from your wife, or a handmade cigar box from your grandfather will hold more value. This is because they move us emotionally. By putting thought into your gifts, you are sharing your humor, creativity, song, dance, words, personality, and touch. You are inserting yourself and that is always the most valuable part of the gift.

MEN: When women say "it's the little things", this is what they're talking about. Notes. Reminders. Messages, pieces of you, everywhere, scattered during the most unpredictable times. Not only on birthdays and anniversaries, but any day. It's not the gift, it's the thought behind it. Give when you're least expected to. That's when it will hit the hardest. Trust me, she will repay you in other ways. But of course, that is not the reason why you are doing it. If so, you are taking and not giving.

What if I'm not a creative person? You don't have to be. The gift is you so all you have to do is share it. It's about the *how*, not the *what*.

Also, remember that putting thought into your gifts isn't about them. It's about you. A person's gift is telling of the person. This behavior defines you. It creates great stories. Memorable or forgettable is only the result. Putting thought into your gifts is about choosing to be selfish (not sharing yourself) or selfless (sharing yourself). There's only one of you on this planet. Let us experience the rare gift that is you.

WOMEN: If he puts thought into his gifts, whether they are for you or not, please acknowledge it. Tell him how you feel about it. Empower him, encourage him. It is rare to find a man who is generous enough to consider others yet confident enough to share himself.

#12 Do Walk with a Gorilla Chest

I had the opportunity to see a Silverback Gorilla a few years ago when I was working with teenagers in a residential treatment center. He was the most massive, powerful, intimidating animal I've ever seen in my life. His arms were like tree trunks. When he ran toward you, you could feel the ground thunder. But it wasn't the six hundred pounds of muscle that was shit-your-pants frightening. There are bears, elephants, lions, and other animals just as massive. It was his stance, his posture, his body communicating two words, *try me.*

In CrossFit, when you're doing a deadlift, you will hear the coaches screaming gorilla chest! This means push your chest out. Do not round your back or you will lose it. This posture prevents injury, but it also creates power. You are positioning yourself to be filled with certainty. Chest out and up. Your form acts as a sealant that keeps the energy from leaking. You can feel it as it enters your body, in your grip, in the weight of your heels. It's this anchor that allows you to lift more weight than you've ever imagined.

MEN: Do you slip into a room slouched and invisible? Or do you enter like you own the room? You will know by people's reactions. They will either act as though you are wall paper or notice you and instinctively step aside. The way you carry your body is an extension of how you view yourself. There is power in posture. That being said, there is also a difference between posture and posturing. One stems from certainty. The other from seeking approval. If you don't want to be noticed, posture. If you want to lead, walk with a gorilla chest.

WOMEN: Add "gorilla chest" to your check list so that when he grabs your hand and walks this earth, you feel safe. When you meet someone, take in his posture not just his smile. One holds certainty, the other just pretty teeth. But also know that there is a difference between certainty and controlling. One's a knock off. The other is the real deal.

#13 Don't Fart in Front of Your Girlfriend / Wife

I never understood the whole *we're so comfortable we go to the bathroom in front of each other* thing. There are just some things a couple should not do together and this is one of them. Another is drugs. My point is there is a small space of mystery that is necessary for a relationship to be healthy and exciting. Watching each other go to the bathroom does not fit under *small space of mystery*. If that space is eliminated, it will effect the chemistry. Going to the bathroom in front of each other completely washes that space. Once you've crossed that line, you can't go back. What does all this have to do with farting? If going to the bathroom in front of each other is sex, farting is foreplay. Once you start farting, the other is bound to happen. It's just a matter of time. You don't want to open that door.

MEN: I understand you can't help what keeps happening in yoga class or when you're sleeping. I am guilty of this myself. But I'm not referring to something you can not control. I'm talking about men who give their girlfriends "Dutch ovens" and put lighters to their asses. Why add to her list of *Things I will tolerate*? Shouldn't you be trying to rid that list? Respect that space of mystery or you'll wonder why your sex life has become a mystery.

WOMEN: The rules don't change because you are female. We know you do it too. You're just better at hiding it. Also, don't run into the bathroom to pee while we're in the shower. Just because you don't have a penis doesn't make it okay. Unless you want us to imagine you doing what you claim never happens.

#14 Do Sweat Daily

We used to wake up at dawn and spend the day hunting dinner. We used to build our own homes, fetch water, and cut fire wood. We used to make things with our hands, not because it was our job but because it gave us a sense of accomplishment. We used to run, climb, swim, jump, and sweat. And it wasn't called exercise. It was called life.

Today, men cruise in air conditioned cars, ride elevators, and sit in cubicles. They build equity, climb the corporate ladder, and cut corners. This behavior has turned us into machines. Sweating reminds us that we are in fact human. Of course there's obvious health benefits to sweating. It flushes out toxins and disease. It can also aide in improving cardiovascular health. As the body heats and produces sweat, the heart works harder to improve circulation. By regularly working up a good sweat, these benefits can have long-term health benefits. But that is not the reason I believe men should sweat daily.

There is a gift in tasting our own salt. It's a different sense of worth than landing a promotion or closing a deal. It rides on the most basic human level, one stripped of external forces, involving nothing else but you and what God has given you. It's our way of shedding. The after effect is a shot of empowerment. This stimulates self esteem, crushes false beliefs, and generates testosterone - all imperative in the journey of man.

MEN: I understand it's a different time. There's nothing wrong with elevators. But pick up a kettle bell once in a while, take the stairs, walk to the grocery store. Take your dog to the canyons, your iPod to the beach, a jump rope to the park. Be active. Sweat. Prove that you are alive.

WOMEN: Join us in our daily sweat. You've heard that saying, A couple that prays together stays together? Well I believe a couple that sweats together has awesome sex.

There is nothing more attractive than a woman who is comfortable / confident in her body. Sweating daily is a piece of that confusing puzzle advertisers don't want you to put together. Be a diamond. Not a stone.

#15 Do Display Physical Affection

After 39 years, I have yet to see my father display any form of physical affection toward my mother. Let me rephrase that. He has tried to steal kisses as a joke or to get a reaction, primarily for the sake of entertaining his sons. But never a heart touch - A touching of hearts with other parts. Yes, I did just say that. No, I don't care what you think. Back to my dad. No hugs, no kisses, no holding hands, not even a squeeze on the shoulder to remind her she is not alone in this world. Today, they sleep in separate bedrooms. Sometimes I wonder how I was created.

MEN: Relationships are like cell phones. Without full bars, the connection is poor. With poor connection, people drift. Physical affection and touch is one way to keep those bars strong while you're hitting dry patches. Or if you're not. Do you not display physical affection because you're embarrassed? If that's the case, you're with the wrong person or you seek too much approval. No? That's not it? Oh, you're just not a touchy feely person? And where do you think you learned that from? This behavior is a virus that will be passed down through the generations. Unless someone stops it. Break the cycle. Something as simple as a hand on a shoulder or a palm on a back, validates, confirms, and assures that you are present - investing in this relationship.

WOMEN: Seek men who can't keep their hands off you, especially outside the bed room. Every man knows women like and appreciate some form of physical affection. If he says he doesn't, tell him. Give him examples. Basic hand holding while you're walking, shoulder rubs during a movie, knee squeezes in the car, you get the drift. If after you have told him you would like this and he is resistant, it may mean he is seeking approval from others, not feeling confident in self, or as Greg Behrendt would say, *he's just not that into you.*

Yes, it can also be a cultural thing. But if he lives in America, that is not an excuse. If he's uncomfortable with it because it wasn't modeled in his family, that only buys him a chance to change.

#16 Do Things Alone

As important as it is to spend time with our friends, girlfriend, co-workers, and family, we must also spend time alone. Masturbation and overtime does not count. When I say alone, I mean things that allow us to know and discover ourselves. Women define "me" time as activity that is therapeutic on some level, clears the head, resets the body, and reboots them as an individual. Activities may include a day at the spa, salon, or mall. Or at a shooting range, mountain side, or race track. For us, it may be golfing, having a beer with the boys, or a trip to Costa Rica. But those activities aren't usually done alone. The difference between men and women is the mindset. Men don't usually do things by themselves as a way to reflect, unless they're going through a crisis. And even then, it will probably involve friends. If they do things alone, it's more about the activity and less about the process. Women, on the other hand, enjoy the process. It's a mental bath. They crave it. They need it. But find it difficult because they are constantly harassed by men when doing it. Because well, we don't like to be alone.

The other purpose of doing things alone is to feel comfortable with ourselves. It is imperative for a man to possess this type of comfort. It bleeds through other areas of his life. It builds confidence. Raises one's differentiation of self. He will seek less from others and have a stronger sense of who he is. Simply put, he won't have to cling to his girlfriend at a party.

MEN: When's the last time you went to a movie by yourself? Ate dinner in a restaurant alone? Went out on a Friday solo? Doing things alone doesn't make you a loser. It makes you healthy. If you feel discomfort when you are doing things alone, explore it. Where does it come from? Do you feel self conscious? Are you worried about what others will think of you? The stronger your alone muscles, the less likely you will be alone.

WOMEN: Look for the guy that's reading in the corner by himself, enjoying coffee and pie at the end of the counter, standing alone in front of a painting. For he is the one that will give you space, embrace your independence, appreciate your company, and ultimately be the leader you are looking for.

#17 Do Keep Your Bathroom Clean

If the kitchen is your heart, the bedroom your soul, the bathroom is your character. This means we will be judged on it. She will glance at our kitchen, eye our appliances, maybe peek in our fridge to see what we put in our body. But her observation stems more from a curiosity standpoint than one of judgement. It would be like us checking out her entertainment station, movies, games, music, etc. The bedroom, now that she will take in. There's a difference between observing and taking in. When you take something in, you are using all your senses. She will notice the smell, the energy. She will notice if the bed is made, if there's dirty socks on the floor. She may even sit on the bed. And if she does, that is a good sign. The bathroom, this one she will dissect. Partly because she will be in there alone. But more because it is telling of who you are. She will go though your products, colognes, lotions, notice your towels, the toilet, if it's clean and the seat is up, anything displayed on the walls. Photos, art, knick knacks. She will put on her detective hand and her eyes will turn into a black light. This means she will be able to see things we don't. Like that strand of hair in the drain, the runny shampoo bottle, and the light hint of urine. She is now taking this information and applying it to her life, wondering if she can live with someone like this. Or change them.

All that being said, the point of keeping our bathroom clean isn't to impress women. It about shaping behavior that bleeds to other areas of our life. A clean bathroom means a clean state of mind. The "do" here doesn't mean to do it once. It means to keep it clean, always. That is where behavior is formed, patterns are broken, and growth is possible.

MEN: Here's the good news. They don't expect to eat off the floor. They just want to know you're not in college anymore.

WOMEN: We know you go through our shit.

#18 Do Eat at the Same Pace as Your Company

I remember the daggers she shot at my thirteen year old friend, Charlie, who was sitting right next to me with a tense face. He leaned forward toward her and mumbled through his clenched teeth, "you better not". I knew they were talking about me, the little neighborhood Korean kid they invited for dinner that evening. But I didn't know what the big secret was. I wondered if there was something on my face. As she bit her tongue and went back to her Spaghetti, it hit me like the end of "The Sixth Sense". Instantly I retrace all the looks thrown at me from Charlie's family during dinner. The averted eyes. The stares. The tight lips while chewing. It had nothing to do with my face. It was my mouth. I forgot to close it while I was chewing.

Fortunately, family dinners, proms, weddings, business brunches, and a shit load of dates will eventually train you proper eating etiquette if your parents didn't or you grew up in a culture where eating with your mouth open was acceptable. Of course, it comes at the expense of some social trauma. But even if you eat with your lips sealed and hold the correct fork, posture, and glass, you most likely will slip on one thing, pace.

MEN: We eat faster than women. We just do. I don't know if it's nature or nurture. I just know that when you put something in front of us, whether it's to build or consume, we go at it as fast as we can. But here's the thing. If we're focused on our food, we are not focused on her. This means we are not sharing the moment. The meal becomes a task instead of an experience. It's not only rude, it's bad for you. Slow down. Chew.

WOMEN: Again, it's all about behavior. If he's solely focused on fulfilling his needs without considering you, what else does he do this way?

#19 Put Your Phone Down

It all started with the pager. This little vibrating gizmo was more than a connection device, it made us feel important. Every time our hip vibrated, we saw our "Bat symbol" in the sky. We felt wanted and needed. Some of us had two of them, one for business and one for personal use. People noticed them. We liked that people noticed them. It made us feel powerful.

Then came cell phones. They were big and expensive. It was a luxury to have one. It meant we had money or were in the process of making it. It gave us attention as well as a voice. People noticed them. We liked that people noticed them. It made us feel powerful.

Once cell phones became mainstream, it was less about how it made us feel and more about what we could do with it. Technology turned our Pseudo Self Solid. We weren't trying to sell anymore. Instead, we were bought.

Today, we can't function without these little devices. We are on them constantly. Work, home, car, gym, lunch, bathroom, and on dates. We if lose it or leave it at home, instant panic sets in. They keep us connected to the world. But the truth is, they keep us trapped in our own bubble.

MEN: On the surface, being on your smart phone when you're in the presence of company is a rude ritual. You are posturing or your mind is somewhere else, or both. You are not giving the other person your undivided attention. But this is not just about being respectful to your company. It's about man vs. machine. These devices are supposed to connect us but they are actually pulling us apart. We'd rather type than talk.

It gives us a way to hide, avoid. We lose a generation in our communication. Instead of using it as a tool, we are using it as a clutch. We must put the phone down and look into eyes instead of screens. We must tame our machines. Own them before they own us. We must respect our kind. Or we will have no one to text.

WOMEN: By putting his phone away, he is shutting off the world for you. Hopefully, you are doing the same. If he doesn't, instead of taking out your own device, ask him to put his away. Remember, we're on the same team.

#20 Don't Be Creepy

Creepy is like Halitosis. It comes from within. It is an energy that leaks from pores that women can smell like sharks smell blood. I believe this energy stems from a fear that stems way back to a lonely childhood and a lack of strong male role models. Men creep because no one ever taught them healthy boundaries, how to confront, address, or look people in the eyes. They never learned the value of courage.

Creepy manifests from a false belief that one is not good enough = fear of rejection = a form of fight or flight. Fight or flight means rubbing against women in dark clubs, stalking on Facebook, driving by the coffee shop to make sure she is with who she said she would be with, and of course, over thinking everything.

MEN: First, know that creepy repels women more than Ed Hardy shirts. Second, know that you can't just stop being creepy. You may be able to plug the hole temporarily but there will eventually be another leak. Don't kid yourself. Creepy is ingrained. In order to stop, you must explore your wiring, your fear, and begin a process of acceptance, validating, and loving self. Simply put, you must grow.

WOMEN: When you run into someone who's being creepy, imagine them as Peter Pan. They are adult children. Know that they are immature, not evil. It's a behavior from lacking tools. I understand that doesn't make you any more attracted to them, but understanding allows empathy. My wish is that you empathize instead of criticize. Use their stunted growth to promote yours.

#21 Don't give her everything she wants. Do give her everything she needs.

The key word here is "everything". Of course you should try to give her things she wants like romantic dinners, thoughtful notes hidden inside her purse, and surprise concert tickets to her favorite band, assuming that giving is not due to fear of losing her or her loving you less. If you are focused on giving because of fear, you are actually not giving. You are taking. You are seeking approval or validation in exchange for your gift. It's in this state that you slip into giving her "everything". It may be your definition of a good boyfriend or husband. But what you don't realize is that you are becoming a "yes man", losing your spine, going from her mouth to her nipple. We give everything because we are afraid. And this fear will change the chemistry. You will feel it in the bedroom.   She won't trust you because of this fear. Women are like vines. They need a wall, not Jello. It is impossible to give everything without losing yourself.

On the other hand, you should try to give her everything she needs. Things she needs? Honesty, trust, respect, support, empathy, communication, undivided attention, a space that allows her to feel beautiful. Those are just a few. Ask her for the full list.

MEN: It's all about the intent. When you give, ask yourself if you are truly giving or taking. Make sure the giving is coming from an honest place.

The way you give her her "needs" is what will set you apart from the rest. Only YOU can give them to her in that way. Know this. This is why it's important for you to know yourself, your gifts, what you bring to the table, what makes you you. If you don't know, neither will she.

WOMEN: Tell your man what you need. Don't make it a guessing game and judge him on it. Let it be an exercise to be heard. If you don't allow yourself to be heard, neither will he.

#22 Do Dance (Especially if You Don't Know How)

Put us in a situation where we may look foolish and our response will determine how comfortable we are with ourselves.

Ever since we were kids, men have been programed to capture the flag. Our competitive streak is etched with permanent ink. If we believe we can't do something, we tend to avoid it. The dancing flag sits very high on a steep mountain that most men aren't willing to climb. Not that we don't want to. Fear of looking stupid (failure) keeps us from embarking on that journey.

MEN: What women find attractive isn't your ability to do headspins or a fancy Charleston. If you can, great. She will be entertained, as she would if she was watching a good magic trick. But she won't be as impressed as if you danced without knowing how. The reason is one requires much more courage than the other. And this ability to be fearless, to not care what others think, is what is sexy.

My encouragement for you to dance, especially if you don't know how, isn't to capture a woman's eye. It's to get comfortable with the uncomfortable. In this space is where you will find growth. Of course, dancing isn't the only activity that brings discomfort to men. But I do believe it's one of the most common and challenging.

WOMEN: Don't tell the men but yes, dancing is sexy. It's not like watching magic tricks. I know. I just said that so they won't compare themselves to Justin Timberlake or Fred Astaire. I understand the way a man moves his body can be something you replay over and over in the tub.

My point is this: find a man who is willing to look foolish and you will not only find a confident man, but a fun one, because Will Ferrel is just as sexy as Justin Timberlake. Right? Wait, don't answer that. Let me rephrase. There's nothing sexier than a man willing to make a complete ass of himself.

#23 Do Go on Man Dates

Just as I roll up to a fresh red light, he pulls up right next to me, pops his helmet window open, and asks casually as if we've been chatting at a coffee shop for hours, "How do I get her to give better head?". I pop my face mask up and yell, "You gotta tell her what you like and don't like". He thinks about this. "I've never had to give instructions before. How do I even know what's good?" I think about this for a second before replying, "You know it's good when she forgets you're attached to it." The light turns green. We slap our masks down and shoot forward once again.

It started as a "Let's catch up". We decided to meet at a local burger joint on our motorcycles. The thought of watching the sun sink with a gas tank in between my legs seemed like the perfect way to end a long Thursday. Over burgers and fries, we talked about women and relationships. I reminded him to keep his bar high, to seek someone who will bring out his best. He needed this reminder.

Next stop was frozen yogurt. We sat on the ledge licking our giant waffle cones like kids allowed to hang out alone for the first time, our bikes parked right next to us. Now the conversation was about work and our frustration with our careers, where we are now versus where we want to be. We expressed our fears and supported each other in ways only men can.

By the time we were riding back, the topic turned into sex as it always does. But our conversation happened in fragments in between traffic lights. The night ended with bear hugs. It was needed. We left lighter than when we had arrived.

MEN: Going on man dates isn't about burgers, sex talk, or motorcycles. It's about being in the trenches together, building another space for growth which doesn't take away from the one you and your girlfriend/wife share. It's a different space. You get something out of your boys that you can't from your girl. It's healthy and needed. This process sharpens us and reminds us that we are men. So if you want to be the best man you can be, make your man date a mandate.

WOMEN: I know it's hard to hear, but there are just some things you can't give us. One of them is the support and comradery we get from other men. If you do everything in your power to cock block this, not only will you earn the title "dragon lady", but you will also be stunting your boyfriend/husband's growth. Spending time with his boys doesn't mean he doesn't want to spend time with you. It just means he wants to spend time with his boys. At the end of the day, what he gets will only make him a better friend, father, and husband.

#24 Do Be Humble

The common thread in all great leaders is humility. The reason is when we are humble, we are open. There is space for self understanding, awareness, and reflection. We have a suggestion box. With this box comes responsibility. Accepting this responsibility brings us down from our pedestal. Unity is formed which then builds trust. Trust allows people to feel safe. Cohesion is created. With this glue, the group, partnership, marriage, company, classroom, CrossFit box, nation is ready to be lead, move forward, and change.

If we are self centered, we are closed. We are cement. There is no discussion. Only pointed fingers. We sit high, looking down. This does not allow space for self understanding or awareness. Without this space, there is no opportunity to be responsible. No responsibility means no unity which means no trust. People feel unsafe. The container is cracked. There is no growth.

Humility is trusting.

Arrogance is threatening.

We all have an ego. To check that ego is difficult. It goes against our human nature. It means accepting that we are not perfect. Since many associate perfect with power, they think humility equals weakness. But it is the complete opposite. Only when we have accepted our imperfections can we be truly powerful.

MEN: When you think about all the men you respect and admire in this world, how many of them display a sense of superiority, preach instead of teach, put themselves first, brag, talk at you instead of to you? You may respect and admire someone's ability but that does not mean you respect and admire them. There is a difference. Only one is a leader.

WOMEN: I think many mistake humility with not being confident. Don't mistake the two. A man who listens more than speaks, observes first, and responds instead of reacts, may appear insecure and not sure of himself. But that's not the case. He is actually being open. This ability requires courage. If you did which equals confidence. So don't confuse humility with insecurity. A humble man is a confident man.

#25 Do Things That Make You Feel Alive

The five seconds after a crushing CrossFit WOD. A life changing conversation. Make up sex. Heights. The company of a beautiful woman. Swimming in the ocean. Revelations about myself. Giving birth to an idea. That moment when she kisses you back. Running down hill. The first sip of hot coffee in the morning. A broken heart. Writing. An ocean swim. A motorcycle. The birth of an idea. The decision to execute it.

These are some of the things that make me feel alive.

What are yours?

The difference between feeling good and feeling alive is fear. We are not afraid of things that make us feel good. A safe job, a comfortable relationship, twenty minutes on a treadmill. These things don't require much effort. We are not afraid of them. But if you want to feel alive, there must be an element of fear. We might get injured. We might lose money. We might be rejected, labeled, or fired. We might be wrong. But with risk comes reward. Feeling good is not enough. It keeps us trapped in a bubble. Good falls on our lap. Alive doesn't. If we want to feel alive, we must chase it or we will start to feel dead.

MEN: The monotony of your daily life combined with the pressures from work and relationships can put you in an emotional coffin. If you want to break out, you must seek what pumps your heart. From the moment you wake up to the second you fall asleep. Little things, big things, it doesn't matter. It's not about the activity. It's about the process of facing your fears.

Ask that girl out. Stand up to your boss. Publish a book. Start a blog. Pick up a guitar. Eat something you wouldn't. Go somewhere foreign. Get out of your comfort zone. Explore your edges. Turn your dial from good to alive. This stretch will change your life. Shatter the fishbowl you live in. If you're content with good, content is all you'll ever be.

WOMEN: Men who do things that make them feel alive have a thirst for life. They are spontaneous, fun, and courageous. These are tools that produces joy and ultimately a happier life. If you want your life to be a ride, seek a pilot. Not a passenger.

#26 Don't Speak to Children Like They're Children

When we speak to children like they're children, instead of bringing them up we are bringing ourselves down. Children look to us to learn, emulate, and grow. If we are acting like them, what are they learning?

MEN: Who was your favorite uncle as a kid? Why was he your favorite? Yes, there was his Trans Am, wild hair, and all the junk food he bought you without telling your parents. But it was also because he treated you like a friend, not a kid. That made you want to hang with him. He didn't talk down to you or baby you. You felt respected and important. He bought you up to his level instead of dropping down to yours. You appreciated this. He was the only one that made you feel like an adult. Give this gift to children.

WOMEN: The way a man acts around children, especially yours, is a great measure of how comfortable he is with himself. Observe him around five year olds. Is he acting in a way he thinks he should act or is he just being himself? Is he trying to earn points or give them? Also, watch how they act around him. Children are transparent which means they call bullshit. They will either find him comfortable or annoying. They will either cling or cringe. And eventually, so will you.

#27 Don't Be a Bully

Bullies aren't just angry kids on the playground.
They're grown adults. They run companies, wear
uniforms, and raise families. They exist at work,
home, and church. You may be be sleeping with one.
The act of bullying comes in many forms, not just
physical. There is emotional bullying, financial
bullying, spiritual bullying, and mental bullying to
name a few. Ultimately, a bully is someone who tries
to take away one's power so that they can feel like
they have more. For them, this feeling of being
powerless creates fear and it's this fear that drives
them to be manipulative, controlling, aggressive, and
abusive. Simply put, bullies are cowards. They are
afraid to face their own defects and deficiencies, so
they make others aware of their own.

MEN: Bullies were bullied. Break the cycle. You're
not bad. You're hurt. If you want to start the healing
process, you have to stop the bullying. This behavior
does not make you powerful. It makes you
powerless. Take the power back by taking
responsibility for your actions and how they impact
others.

WOMEN: Impulsive. Afraid. Angry. Confused.
Controlling. Cowardice. Lonely. Mean. Careless.
Heartless. Hurt. Needy. Predictable. Attention
seeking. Arrogant. Weak. Insecure. Insensitive.
Unaware. Jealous. Abusive. Violent. Aggressive.
Selfish. Are these the qualities you are seeking in a
husband, father, or friend?

#28 Do Walk Your Talk

Words without action are just words.

MEN: Every time you don't do what you said you would, you are creating a crack in the relationship. Any relationship, with your boss, friend, or wife. Enough of these cracks and eventually there will be a break. When there is a break, it's not just trust that is broken. It is also your character. Therefore, merely changing your behavior doesn't necessarily equal glue. You have to earn trust but also rebuild your character. How important is your character to you?

A man's word is not everything. It's only half at best. It's his actions that will define him. You can talk all you want. If you don't back it up with action, you will eventually be talking to yourself.

WOMEN: Seek a man who announces less and does more. Seek a man who places value on his words by following through in action. Seek a man that walks his talk.

#29 Do Make Decisions

Nothing cringes female faces more than a man who can't make decisions. The guy who doesn't know where to go on a date, spends half an hour staring at the menu, and asks for permission to kiss.

Ambivalence repels trust like flipped magnets. Without this trust, there is no chemistry, no attraction, and no growth. She may not agree with your decision but must trust that you have the ability to make one. Without this ability, she knows there is no movement. No movement means no journey and she is seeking a man on a mission. Not a boy lost at sea. Simply put, if you can't make decisions, you're not going anywhere.

MEN: The ability to make a decision is a tool. It allows you to be heard, have a voice, and build trust. Not only with her but with yourself. The action of making a decision paves you a road. The pattern of these decisions will determine what kind of road you are on. It will remind you who you are and where you are going. It's better to choose and be wrong than not choose at all. If you don't pull the trigger, you will lose your gun. So pick a lane, a side, a color. Choose a restaurant, a woman, a cause. Your decisions will define your character. Make a choice or you will be in the ocean instead of on a road.

WOMEN: Making decisions doesn't mean being controlling. One stems from a belief in self. The other, insecurity. Don't mistake the two. One allows growth and the other stunts it.

#30 Do Laugh Hard

There are two types of people in this world. People who laugh, and people who laugh hard. People who laugh hard live in the moment. They seek nectar. They are spontaneous. They are adventurous. They are committed. They are courageous. They are confident. They have a thirst for life. They are leaders.

I've always been insecure about my smile. So I grew up being the "I smile with my eyes" or "I laugh on the inside" guy, which is just another way of saying I'm insecure. It's a form of hiding. It made me feel like the odd man out. I hated that I couldn't laugh like everyone else, that I didn't have the courage to. Today, when I feel that rumbling and my face start to pull, I remind myself to commit like a gymnast doing backflips. I push through, let go, and laugh as hard as I can.

MEN: The reason why women love guys who laugh and smile isn't solely because they look good doing it. It's because they are displaying vulnerability. They are showing the world that they can be confident and happy without announcing it. They are expressing themselves and choosing to share it with others, which allows others to feel something. So if you're going to laugh, do it fearlessly; life is too short to just laugh.

WOMEN: Don't settle for men who are afraid to laugh.   They are approval seekers and followers. More importantly, they are boring.   Find someone who has permanent laugh lines.   The deeper the better.   They're like rings on a tree but instead of a measure of age, see them as a fun meter.   Laughter is contagious.   Ask yourself how much fun you want to have in your life before you get involved with a man who is afraid to laugh.

#31 Don't Be Afraid of Women

Models are lonely. What do you think about that statement? Sound ridiculous? Based on my observations and conversations working with models on an internet reality show back in my twenties, I learned that many do not get asked out as much as one would think. Don't "beautiful people" have a waiting list? Aren't they in high demand? Doesn't everyone want to be with them? Possibly, but the truth is we are also intimidated by them. Everyone has a fear of rejection, but men struggle with society's ideas and the pressure of A), having to be the pursuer, meaning they are expected to approach the woman. And B), what it means if she says "no". The locker room has added an internal pressure to close the deal. If we don't, we may internalize her disinterest as failure, one of our greatest fears.

MEN: Here's the catch 22. The more we fear women, the greater the chance they will reject us since fear is something that repels them. The more often we are rejected, the greater our fear will grow. We must break this cycle. The bad news is we can't fake courage. They can smell it a mile away. You have to genuinely not be afraid. This means you have to know yourself and be okay with who you are. This is a process. Not something you learn in a "how to pick up women" seminar.

Here's a tip. When you see a stunning woman you are afraid to approach, know that she was once just an insecure girl seeking approval. Maybe she still is. Know that she has a story like everyone else. And it's not perfect. My point is look pass the skin. Talk to her heart.

WOMEN: Men objectify women when they are afraid of them. It's easier to accept rejection from an object than a real human being. So the next time you feel objectified, know that his words and behavior is stemming from fear. Accepting this will give him a heart and stretch yours.

#32 Don't Over Use Hair Product

In the 50's, we used grease. The 80's, hair spray. The 90's, gel. Today, pomade? The good news is we look less manufactured. The bad news is we are still putting way too much stuff in our hair. Hair is important. I get it. It shapes our face and makes us feel young. But the more effort we put into molding our hair into the perfect shape, the louder we are yelling "Look at me!". We all want people to look at us. But we don't want to announce it. It screams insecurity. The goal is to not be concerned with what others think. If we can't do that, then we must look the part. The way we do this is by appearing as natural as possible. Natural doesn't mean boring. It means pure. Honest.

MEN: We are concerned with how things looks. Women are more concerned with how things feel. This means they would rather be able to run their hands through your hair than stare at it.

WOMEN: You're welcome.

#33 Do Seek Nectar

Decipher thought all that is manufactured, programmed, and contrived. Break monotony by wearing new lenses, ones that allow you to explore edges and find truth in moments. Seeking nectar means to simplify, look closer, and find life in your life. In order to do this, you must live inside out. You must pull from your Solid Self instead of Pseudo. You must address and validate yourself. You must find meaning.

I used to be a miserable fuck. I was obsessed with chasing rainbows instead of finding meaning in what was in front of me. I was absent in relationships and always in my head. I wasn't in life. I was in line. Being in line makes you powerless. Living without power makes you angry. In order to get that power back, I had to change my mindset. I didn't have a choice. It was either that or continue to be miserable and powerless. I decided to not focus on the destination but rather the journey. I got out of line. I went back to school. I changed careers. I started a blog. I realized that life is not about waiting. It's about giving. But we can't give until we know what our gifts are. In order to do that, we must take what's in front of us, moments, relationships, events, situations, tragedies, and find truth and meaning (nectar) in them. In truth, you will find lessons. In meaning, you will find purpose.

MEN: Quit waiting in line. Stop wasting your gifts. Seek nectar, always, in everything you do. It doesn't matter if you're doing the dishes, on a date, or building an empire, this mindset will allow you to be open, aware, and unlock your code so that you can unleash your gifts. The world needs you. You were meant to change it.

WOMEN: Roses are not enough. Men who seek nectar live. They are driven. They are thirsty. They are leaders. Raise the bar. Set your standard. Seek men who seek nectar and you will find a man who is not just living, but actually alive.

#34 Do Eat Something Green

My journey with food has been a rocky one. I was raised on fast food. My parents owned burger stands and fast food franchises while I was growing up. Fried chicken for breakfast. Egg rolls and chili fries for lunch. Tacos for dinner. Fast food was always just a "call before mom leaves" away. This meant two things. One, a lot of friends as a kid. Two, an unhealthy habit which would lead to many heated arguments later in life between my inner adult and child.

Today, I still struggle with my desire for processed and fried. But it doesn't have the control over me like it once did. I have learned to tame my desires, to not let my wants overthrow my needs. I have finally learned the concept of control. Simply put, I have grown.

One overlooked element that distinguishes a boy from a man is his diet. Boys consume only what tastes good. Men eat what tastes good but also what they believe is good for them. Eating solely what tastes good is a reaction, not a response. It is an impulsive action. Eating what is good for you requires thought and discipline.

It is a response to your body needing nourishment. There is maturity in that decision and strength in the ability to execute it. Boys react. Men respond. That being said, all in moderation. There's nothing wrong with pizza and milk shakes as long as it's not the only thing you consume.

MEN: It's time to look at food as fuel. Respect your body. Reset your mind. It's time to find healthier ways to cope. It's time to have control over your cravings. It's time to eat something green.

WOMEN: It's not about the food. It's about his mindset, which bleeds into other areas of his life. A man's diet is a direct reflection on his self control, impulse, and how much he loves himself.

#35 Do Separate What You Do From Who You Are

As society places worth on women by their appearance, it places worth on men by their ability. What you can build, how many home runs you can hit, money you can make all define a man's worth. We internalize this definition and believe that if we are bad at something, we are worth less. On the other hand, if we are good at something, we are worth more. Both are false. They are labels. Our worth has nothing to do with what we can do. By thinking this way, we run the risk of losing ourselves and what we truly have to offer. We forget about the other aspects of us that make us whole, our soul, our spirit, and our capacity to love.

MEN: Your drive, passion, and ambition are all great gifts. Your athletic ability, your voice, your ability to lead, create, and change the world are imperative to your journey. But they do not determine your worth. Your value comes in who you are, not what you can do. Your character and heart make you you.

WOMEN: Men that are really good at what they do are attractive. I get that. But look deeper. People that are great at something get praised for it. It's quite easy for their ability to become their identity. Like income, performance fluctuates which means their self worth will go up and down. Seek consistency by seeking men who can separate what they do from who they are. Because it's who they are that will get you through the rough patches of your relationship, not what they can do.

#36 Do Call People by Their Names

Dear Male Server,
When I am eating out alone, please don't refer to me as "dude", "buddy", or "bro". Your desire to seek an instant connection makes me feel like I'm in college again. I believe your behavior stems from your resistance to feeling subservient, which really means you're unhappy with your job. By achieving this connection, you will feel less subservient and better about what you do. Suddenly you're my friend and not the guy that brings me bread and refills my passion fruit ice tea. I get that. I was a server once too. I am sorry you are unhappy with your job. Really, I am. I know what it feels like to do something you dread. I've been there. I've even been fired for not being good at it. But by calling me these things, it creates more of a disconnection than a connection. It's forced, false. You are putting up a wall. If you want to connect, be you, be real. Say you're having a bad day and I'll tell you about mine. Say you hate your job and I'll share the time I wore a radio active jump suit and peeled plasma in a factory for minimum wage one summer. Say the meatloaf is not edible and my stomach will thank you. That will earn you respect and the connection you are seeking. Once we have this connection, there will be an exchange. This exchange may remind you that your job isn't that bad because you made an authentic connection. But more importantly, you gave the gift, which is you. And you may will realize that you are not what you do.

MEN: Nick names have to be earned in order for them to mean anything. If you don't know someone, call them by their actual name. Once you get to know them, tagging an alternative can be a seal instead of a crowbar. If we want to sharpen each other, we must respect each other first. My name is John Kim. If you are a friend, you might call me JK, Chools, Special K, or Korean Monkey.

WOMEN: If he doesn't call people by their names, call him out. Remind him. Let him know that it's disrespectful. Tell him it doesn't make him cute. It makes him afraid. Also, if someone you don't know refers to you as "honey", "sweetie", "sweetheart", or "hey", turn to them, offer your hand with a smile and give them your name. They will not be expecting this. They will be expecting you to be afraid. Flip the script. Turn the table. Suddenly, *they* will be afraid. Introduce yourself. Show them what fearless looks like.

#37 Do Have the Mindset of an Athlete

My dance with Crossfit has introduced me to a sea of athletes. They are not athletes because of how much weight they can lift over their head or how many unbroken burpees they can do. They are athletes because they posses a freight train determination. They have a desire to earn something. They set goals. They are honest with themselves. They push others. They don't complain. They don't cheat. They don't whine. They don't hide. They have a thirst for life and seek change. They accept challenges. They seek improvement. They are mothers, fathers, brothers, and daughters. They deliver your mail, take your food order, and invest your money. They are "average" people with exceptional character, who just happen to run five minute miles and hang power snatch two hundred and twenty five pounds. Athlete doesn't mean performance. It means character. If you have amazing athletic ability but no character, you are not an athlete. You are just athletic.

MEN: I encourage you to have the mindset of an athlete even if you are not athletic. This is the recipe for success. The vicious cycle of fearless drive, failure, and getting back up again with integrity is the set up and pay off that causes momentum and allows you to create ripples in this world. Men, ability can be a gift or a curse. Character is the deciding factor.

WOMEN: We are not born with this mindset. It is a choice and a process, an extremely difficult one. It requires fighting ego, insecurities, and our insatiable desire to compare ourselves to others. If you see it, support it, embrace it, acknowledge it. Know the value in having this kind of mindset and how it can affect your children.

#38 Do Travel

Most people leave home when they graduate high school. They go away to college, live in dorms, study abroad. I lived with my parents and commuted to a university thirty minutes away. I could blame it on my culture since Korean children are expected to live at home until they get married. The truth was travel wasn't important to me. I saw it as recreation, as extra, as play. If you leave, you're wasting valuable time. Someone else is getting ahead while you're buying souvenirs. Ambition kept me in a bubble.

Beat.

Okay, the real truth was I was afraid. I was scared to leave my cocoon. I was a closed person and didn't have the courage to explore the unknown. It took many years of excuses but finally, at 37, I took the plunge. I traded my "motorcycle money" for two weeks in Italy and Barcelona. I figured if I got the bike first, I may not have legs. This trip was my little red ice cream shop taster spoon of travel. I had pizza where it was invented. I stood in front of art I learned about in text books. I rode scooters. I swam in the Mediterranean Sea. I saw beautiful people. I had conversations with strangers. I met a girl. I walked. I danced. I drank. I explored. I lived.

MEN: Any opportunity you get to travel, take it. Life doesn't allow us to go anywhere. We have to make it happen. Don't wait like me to get your taster spoon. Order a cone, a giant waffle cone. It will be filled with knowledge, perspective, acculturation, substance, discovery, and growth. It will open your mind, stretch your heart, and allow you to see.

WOMEN: Men who travel have more practice with patience. The act of travel can be tedious. Dealing with other cultures, sensitivity, communication, requires one to strengthen the patience muscle. Men who travel have a better understanding of people. They experience other languages, rituals, societies, foods, music, art, business, living, and production. Men who travel are more open. They have the ability to adjust, adapt, see the world through other people's eyes. A well traveled man is a wise man.

#39 Don't Spray Cologne Directly on You

Walk into it instead.

MEN: Women have a stronger sense of smell than we do. This means if you can detect a hint of something, they are smelling it like it's smeared on their nose. Cologne is stronger than you think. Also, you will not be putting your face on or next to it as they will.

She finds your natural scent sexier than any man made fragrance out there. So if you feel the need to use cologne, enhance. Don't cover. I think Jennifer Aniston said it best, "The best smell in the world is that man that you love."

WOMEN: Men are sensitive about their choice in fragrances. If you say it's too strong, chances are he will interpret it as it smells bad = he smells bad. The way you may want to approach this topic is by saying, "Although I like the smell of your cologne, I would rather smell you."

#40 Don't Be Afraid to Say No

One of the greatest mistakes men can make is to become Yes Men. A Yes Man is someone who is constantly focused on pleasing others even when it goes against his own truth. The fear of being unwanted or rejected overrides his opinions, perspective, and stance. He becomes a placater, an enabler, and ultimately a loner.

At work, the inability to say no turns you into a robot. You become a product, dispensable. It's only when you can say "no" that change can occur, respect can be earned, and a difference can be made. A truthful no opens eyes as well as doors.

If you can't say "no" in friendships, you become a driver, a therapist, and possibly a bank. You will be the one they "forgot" to call when there's an event or the first one they call if they need something. Define your friendships instead of allowing them to define you. Get in the picture instead of holding the camera. Say "no" and see who sticks around. The ones that do are friends. The ones that don't aren't. If no one sticks around, you've been saying "yes" way too long.

When we don't have the ability to say no in intimate relationships, we are creating an unsafe space. If you can't hold your ground, she won't trust you. Broken trust means fading chemistry.

MEN: You can not share your gifts if you are afraid. Fear locks your potential, as a boyfriend, husband, boss, employee, father, brother, son, and leader. It is better to speak your truth and be temporarily alone than be muted and permanently lonely.

WOMEN: If you are with a Yes Man, tell him you NEED someone who will say "no" to you sometimes. It is not a want. It is a need, like touch, communication, and eye contact. Tell him how it affects your opinion and feelings toward him. Tell him you need him to lead, not follow. If you want him to say "no", you may have to dish out the first one.

#41 Do Let Go of Her Sexual History

Let's be completely honest. No matter how much we convince ourselves that it won't matter, knowing how many guys she's been with will eat at us like an Ebola virus.

Phase one. We will wonder about their performance and size. Our mind always goes there first. So we'll ask her questions in a fun and curious way to retrieve the information without appearing threatening. She won't know it's a trap. Neither will we. We believe we can handle it. But we can't. She will tell us a few details but nothing more. She's smart and knows how this will play out.

Phase two. We're off to the races. We will begin to compare and compete. We will play sex scenes from her past and fill in the blanks. We will assume, label, and judge. This will leak into the bedroom. There will be a disconnect. She will be confused. We will be angry.

Phase three. We will start to believe that she would rather be with them even though nothing in her behavior or words claim that. But still, we will believe it with ever fiber of our being. She will think we are "fucking crazy" and realize that we are acting like her jealous ex's, which is why she broke up with them.

We are infected and like herpes, there is no cure. It may be dormant but it will always be there right below the surface.

MEN: You have a right to know your lover's sexual history if it's from a health stand point, as she does yours. But you don't have a right to know about her intimate experiences. If she discloses that information, it is a gift, a sign of trust.
It means she feels safe with you and that you are secure enough with yourself that it will not affect you, your opinion of her, or the relationship. That's a lot of trust. Don't shatter it by holding it in your head or over hers. Let. It. Go. It doesn't matter. What matters is that she's with YOU now.

WOMEN: If he keeps probing about your sexual history and wants to know details, exaggerate your numbers. Tell him you've had the biggest, the best, the craziest, the hottest, and you don't think you'll ever get that again. As he gets that serious look in his eyes, drop the jokes and let him how happy you are with him. Instead of a history report, give him a present report. Tell him what you love about him. Validate him as a lover because that's what this is really about. If after this generous gift you have just given him, he is still probing, ask yourself if you really want to be with someone this insecure.

#42 Do Admit When You Are Wrong

Admitting when we are wrong isn't a sign of weakness. It is a sign of strength. It takes courage to acknowledge our mistakes, defects, and short comings.

MEN: Our fear of looking stupid or less than prevents us from growth. If you can't admit when you are wrong, you are unable to reflect. Without reflection, there are no revelations and without revelations, all you have are false beliefs and white knuckles. Swallow your pride and admit when you are wrong. Discuss it, process it, use it to improve yourself and strengthen relationships. Every time you are wrong there is an opportunity for growth. Don't allow your Pseudo Self to steal that from you.

WOMEN: Men who can't admit when they are wrong are basically saying they are refusing to grow. In every relationship, if you're not growing together, you are growing apart. So if you are with a man who won't admit when he is wrong, it's just a matter of time before you out grow him. Plain and simple.

#43 Don't Perform in the Bedroom

As women live with the pressure to be physically attractive, men live with the pressure to perform. Iron fist fathers, determined coaches, and society's definition of success has convinced us that our worth is contingent on our ability. By the time we're in the rat race known as corporate America, we are wired to define our value by titles, bonuses, and corner offices.

We carry this mindset into the bedroom. As women have been brained washed by the media on what beautiful looks like, we have been brainwashed by pornography and frat boys on what a good lover looks like. Our drive to achieve combined with a warped definition of lover equals performance anxiety, frustration, aggression, and ultimately disconnection.

MEN: When you perform in the bedroom, you are making it about you. When you make it about you, you are leaving her out. The act becomes a solo challenge to capture an imaginary flag. Your focus on the scoreboard creates an emotional wall. Instead of intimacy being a shared experience, it becomes a measuring stick. The more you focus on your "stick", the less connection she will feel and the more pressure you will put on yourself. It's a downhill spiral. Instead, use this space to share yourself instead of proving yourself.

WOMEN: Don't mistake performance with passion. You can feel the difference. One is taking. One is giving. Don't allow him to take. If you feel he is performing, stop him. Tell him you are not enjoying it. Tell him you want to be with *him*, not his ego.

#44 Do Tip Well

Calculator Guy, it's fair when you're with a giant party and you're the one everyone's throwing their credit cards at but if you're out on a date or with your wife, put your calculator away. It will crush her glimmer of hope that behind those scientific eyes is an Indiana Jones dying to break out. This "by the book" behavior = safe = boring. Live a little. Put the calculator away. Round up, and do it in your head.

Approval Man, save that extra money for therapy. You will need it when you fall into a deep depression from not being able to go out anymore. When people see you tipping way more than appropriate, they don't think you're rich and successful. They think you're stupid. They know you're not a baller by the Civic you rolled up in.

Folder Boy, servers are more likely to remember the guy that mind fucked them over the guy that didn't tip well. So instead of folding your money to make it look like there's more, just tip what you can and be extra kind and appreciative. That always goes further than cash anyway.

Mr. Ten Percent Man, that five percent isn't going to break you. If it is, order something cheaper or go to a place where gratuity is not expected. These people get paid minimum wage and have to share their tips with busboys and dishwashers. Most are in transition. This means they have dreams. Know that your gratuity is going toward them.

MEN: Tipping well doesn't just refer to the amount. It refers to how you do it. This includes your attitude. Give gracefully. Make it pure, without resentment or regret. Add a note, "You were wonderful", "The service was great". If you're going to give, give. It says a lot about who you are.

WOMEN: When you're with him, his actions reflect the both of you. If you don't like the way he tips, ask him if you can tip also. You are not asking for permission to do something, you are actually hinting to him in a very polite way that you don't approve of the way he is showing gratitude. If he has a problem with that, discuss it. If it's important to you, it should be important to him.

#45 Don't Smoke Pot

There are people who legitimately use marijuana for clinical applications. It may have been prescribed to reduce anxiety, simulate hunger in chemotherapy or AIDS patients, lower intraocular eye pressure, and help with gastrointestinal illnesses. I am not referring to this population.

I am referring to the boys who smoke out daily, cut out Taco Bell coupons, and subscribe to High Times. I am referring to the 30 year old couch potato licking power cheese off his fingers as he plays Guitar Hero.

MEN: It makes you chubby, smelly, and stupid.

WOMEN: "Just on the weekends" or "once in a while" is still smoking. You're either wearing a T-shirt that says "I'm with chubby, smelly, and stupid" or you're not. It's not about the marijuana. It's about the behavior it encourages.

Yes, I understand there is a stereotype tagged with smoking pot. I believe it is unfair but also unavoidable. If you choose to participate in this behavior, you will be stamped. There's no way around it. I believe a part of being a man is being responsible for the image you project.

#46 Don't Take Yourself Too Seriously

When we take what we do seriously, we are honoring our gifts. Our commitment to excel encourages learning, teaching, and leading. This means we are giving.

When we take ourselves seriously, we are announcing that we *are* the gift. There is truth to that. But if this is our focus, no one will be interested. Instead of standing behind a podium, we are stepping onto a stage. Unless your gift is to entertain, no one wants a show. Without an audience, there is no learning, teaching, or leading. This means we are taking.

MEN: Men give. Boys take. If you have to prove to others what you are good at, you may be good at what you do but you are not confident in who you are. If you are not confident in who you are, it will reflect in what you do. You may be good, but you won't be great. To reach your maximum potential, you must be both. So the next time you feel a need to put on a show, use that energy to produce instead of perform. By doing this, you will eventually turn your high school play into a Broadway musical. Without knowing it.

WOMEN: If he believes he is better than others, he probably believes he is better than you and this relationship. It's only a matter of time before you begin to feel this. But this is not just about you or the relationship, it's about doing your part to help turn boys into men so that your son will grow up with mentors instead of bullies. Call his bluff. Check him. If you don't, who will?

#47 Do Be Nice to People in Service

MEN: Below is an opinion from an actual woman who didn't know she was going to be in my book.

Being snobby or rude to someone who is serving you is really unattractive. I have been on dates where the guy seemed to think he would look smart and funny by talking down to the waiter or making unreasonable demands of the staff. This has just the opposite affect and makes me sure not to go on a second date. I think being polite in general is important, but this one sticks out more so to me. I have known plenty of chefs, busboys, waiters, janitors, etc that were very intelligent and brilliant people who happened to be in that job for one reason or another. I actually know a man who has a little chinese take out named Dr. Shu. He got bored of being a physicist and became a take out owner. I used to see dumb jerks talk down to him all the time, not knowing they were speaking to one of the most brilliant people they would ever meet. I worked in a shop with a cook who was a lawyer in Columbia. Sadly, his law degree and years of experience didn't mean diddly when he immigrated to the US, so he was working his way through school again, cooking in a run down kitchen. And even if the waiter or who ever isn't some rocket scientist on the inside, they are still a human being that deserves respect.

- An actual woman.

#48 Do Kiss Like You Mean It

Do you remember your first kiss? Of course you do. You know exactly where you were and what you were wearing. You remember wondering if you should use your tongue, if your braces would cut her, and how long you should keep your eyes shut. But what you remember the most isn't how it went, it's how you felt. The bats in your stomach, the fear in your heart. The feeling you received, the energy you gave back. You don't remember because you were curious. You remember because you wanted it to mean something.

Do you remember your 2,123rd kiss?

Of course you don't.

When we kiss someone new, it's exciting. It's our first conduit into experiencing the other person intimately. We take our time, bathe in it, get lost. Our mindset is set on discovery mode. We are open to explore. Once we're in a relationship, kissing becomes routine. The exploration is over. We use it as a handshake, a hi, a bye, a see ya later. Or a transition. Rarely do we kiss to discover. We forget the meaning behind kissing. Kissing means to express, connect, validate, assure, give, share, and explore. Not only with the other person but with ourself, and since these are ever changing, every kiss is a new experience.

MEN: Hold her face, touch her lips, look into her soul. Kiss her as if nothing else matters, as if time doesn't exist, as if it's the only way you could express yourself. Use it as an emotional thermometer. Kissing is not a means to an end. It is an experience. Each one stands alone.

WOMEN: Kiss him how you want to be kissed. Show. Don't tell. Grab his head, pull his hair, reach deep into his heart with your mouth. Show him how it's done.

#49 Do Be a Mentor

The process of mentoring creates empowerment. No matter where you are in your life, the act of teaching, guiding, and helping another cements your worth. Prove your value by helping another see theirs.

MEN: We must guide, support, and help the next generation of men so that they transition into honest and courageous husbands, fathers, brothers, and friends. We must give them what we did not receive, share our stories in order for them to write better ones. As a man, we have a responsibility to pay it forward.

We naturally become mentors as we get older. Once our children have their own children, we itch for a connection to feel important again. But our desire to pass down stories and the fact that we have a lot of time on our hands makes mentoring more about us. The challenge is to be a mentor while you are young, time is sparse, and you're still trying to write your story. There are very few of these mentors, which is why you will be extremely valuable.

WOMEN: Mentoring is not just an action. It is a mindset. A mentoring man has his dial set on "there are things bigger than me". This mentality softens a man and encourages him to give instead of take, lead instead of follow. Men with mentoring minds are in check. Their desire to teach and set a good example will remind them of who they are and who they want to be.

#50 Don't Judge

Judgement is loaded. When we judge, we are stamping a giant "should" on the person, experience, or situation. Every should is lined with control so judging really means controlling. Or not being able to.

MEN: You want less anxiety in your life? Stop judging everything, everyone, including yourself. Stop judging your moments, your relationships, your experiences, your life. Even if you don't announce it, we feel it. The energy of judgement leaks and pollutes the air. It shows in your face, your eyes, and your fists. You are making things about you and no one wants to be around that kind of person. Judgement does not promote growth. It stunts it. When you judge, you create your own prison.

WOMEN: He judges because he feels incomplete. By criticizing others, he will feel more whole and powerful. This means he lacks completion and is seeking that in others, mostly you. What does this look like? Closed, controlling, and defensive. Being with someone who needs completion is like dating a black hole. They will suck everything out of you. Judgement is not "just an opinion", it is a repellant for growth.

#51 Don't Text Like You're Seventeen

MEN: Use complete sentences. Make sure the words are spelled correctly. Don't over use profanity. Put thought into your message. Don't text just because you are bored and you need something back. Don't text her every two seconds. Don't get mad if you don't get a text back in two seconds. Don't over use happy faces. Don't use "LOL" because you're just trying to make her feel good. Don't sext if it isn't mutual. Make an effort to be creative. Your cell phone can be a powerful tool for foreplay. Melt her with your words.

WOMEN: You will know how he feels about you by the way he texts you. If you're getting nothing but pictures of his penis, he probably doesn't want a relationship. Or doesn't know how to have a healthy one. But if his texts are funny, kind, thoughtful, mysterious, flirty, fun, appropriate, and honest, you mean something to him. More importantly, he has tools.

#52 Don't Ever Use the Word "Fat" When Speaking to Women

MEN: Unless you're referring to your steak, this F word is off limits. Most women automatically internalize this word. It's what I call a boomerang word. No matter where you throw it, it will always comes back to her. Even if you were talking about someone else, your girlfriend or wife will assume you're thinking the same about her. It's not worth the fight. Trust me. Eliminate it from your vocabulary. Women and weight. Oil and water. This will never change.

The best way to encourage weight loss is to model it. Work on your own body. She will notice. Even if it appears like she doesn't. She thinks about her weight every single day. She doesn't need any reminding. Besides, if she loses weight for you, it will come right back on as fast as it went off. Staying healthy and fit is a life style motivated and generated by self. She needs to do it for her. Not for anyone else. Your behavior can either inspire her or discourage her. The choice is yours.

Let the activity of working out be something you guys share together. The process of accomplishing goals and feeling better about yourselves will create another level of intimacy in the relationship. A bond is created when people sweat together. And it doesn't have to be inside a gym. Run, swim, hike, have Sting sex (Tantra), live. Getting in shape together as a couple. Peanut butter and chocolate.

WOMEN: The locker room has programed us to think words like "fat" and "fatass" are funny. We've been pillow fighting with them for so long, we are unaware that they are not pillows but rather bricks. I am not saying this as an excuse. It is a reminder that the word may carry a different weight with your man. Therefore, you must examine his intent. If he uses the word in a playful way, he may think it's a pillow. Correct him. Express how it makes you feel. If he doesn't stop, he knows his pillow is actually a brick and you must ask yourself if your man is actually a boy.

#53 Do Call When You Say You're Going to Call

MEN: The three day rule. The equation that tells us how young we can date. The two perfect sentences we're supposed to text the day after we sleep with her. The last one I just made up. But you were curious, weren't you? Do you know why? You want instructions. You want rules. You want a proven method. The reason is we are unsure of ourselves.

If we try to build a game plan around a relationship (dating is a form of a relationship), we are going into it with a shield, a veneer. This is called false advertising but more importantly we are minimizing our character. We are offering a false version of us, one filled with insecurity. We are not giving fully. Instead, we are taking. We are seeking approval and validation. They don't want you more if you don't call when you say you're going to call, ignore texts, or send them to voicemail. They're not thinking, "Wow, he's really busy and important." They're thinking, "Wow, he's just like everyone else." By trying to stick out, you will blend in. You don't gain any power by pretending to be unavailable. You lose it. You are performing for the other person. They win. Not you. It takes so much energy to play games. Is that really where you want to spend your energy?

WOMEN: Men who follow society's frame work are followers. They are looking for someone to lean on. Find someone who follows through on what he says. A man's word should be important to him. If it's not, how much weight will "I do" carry?

On the flip side, if you are only attracted to men that are or pretend to be unavailable, what does that say about you? Is that really a cycle you want to repeat?

#54 Do Love Hard

Love is not a feeling. It is an action. The action of loving creates a space for the feeling of love to grow. Therefore, we must not look at love as something that is given but something that we earn, hone, practice, learn from, work at, and strengthen.

Imagine the kind of love we would experience if we put as much time and effort into loving someone as we did our careers and bodies. Why is it that we have no trouble putting in extra time in the gym and working overtime at the office, but when it comes to working on our relationships, it's a chore? We only do it when we are forced to. How many people say their going to work on their relationship when everything is great? If you don't love hard, don't complain about your relationship. To love means to work. I say go hard or get out.

MEN: If you're going to love someone, fucking love someone. Love her like there is no one else on the planet. Love like it's a job you can't wait to go to bed and wake up early for. Love without fear, without pride, without judgement, and without expectation. Love is a gift. Not a negotiation. If you are expecting something back, are you truly giving? If you are unable to do these things, loving hard will mean to explore why.

WOMEN: His ability to "love hard" will depend on where he's at in life, the tools he has, and what he's going through. That means every man will have his own version of loving hard. Do not compare. What's important is his effort. Not his version.

#55 Don't Place Her on a Pedestal

I used to believe that being a "good husband" meant to put her first, above myself. Always. I thought that's what it meant to give completely. Besides, love means sacrifice. Right? Yes, but there is a difference between sacrifice and self sacrifice. In one, you are giving. In the other, you are taking.

MEN: When we sacrifice, we are compromising, bending, and sharing. When we sacrifice self, we are disconnecting, breaking, and seeking something from the other person we lack in ourselves. This process shifts chemistry. We are no longer a wall. We become the vine. When we self sacrifice, we sacrifice the relationship.

Women want to be trusted, adored, loved, appreciated, held, heard, understood, and pampered. But they also want to be challenged, checked, called out, sharpened, and lead. They want you to do life with them, not for them.

WOMEN: When you wake up one day, turn to his drooling face and feel like he's more like a brother than a boyfriend, it's time to have a conversation using first names. During breakfast when he tucks in your bib, you must tell him the chemistry is changing. He will ask you what he's done wrong and how he can fix it. Look him dead in his eyes and say "It's not what you did, it's who you are". This will crush him. He may drop his spatula. Watch your toes. Then explain to him how he makes you feel, and how making it all about you has caused you to trust him less. He will look extremely confused. Make sure he understands. Drive it home. It will be difficult since he will sob like an infant. But he needs to hear this.

Like a broken bone, he will grow back stronger. Hopefully. If not, at least you did your piece and won't feel guilty while your new boyfriend is licking your "famous" pancake batter off your fingers.

#56 Don't Assassinate Character

We assassinate one's character when we don't have enough courage or tools to fight fair. We're using a gun instead of gloves. Assassinating one's character is a form of bullying.

John Gottman, known for predicting divorce with over 90 percent accuracy, spent his career studying how people fought. Character assassination was one of the deciding factors in determining if a marriage would last.

MEN: Apologies won't bring back the character you have assassinated. There is no undo. If you continue to kill her character, she will drift. You may not know how far since her low self esteem / fear of losing the relationship will keep you in the dark or unaware of the damage. This internalization and holding feelings inside will lead to her unhappiness. Eventually, she will seek help. "Help" will allow her to process her anger and resentment. She will begin to have revelations. Her self worth will rise as her false beliefs dissolve and eventually she will go through a rebirth. Simply put, she may not have the strength now. But when she does, she will be gone.

WOMEN: Character assassination is a giant red flag with flashing lights blinking "emotional abuse". This means you are in an abusive relationship. But you say, "When it's good, it's really good. He's going through a lot right now. And he has apologized for everything he's said and done." That's not growth. That's called a cycle. You must break it. He won't. But in order to break it, you must first acknowledge what this is, abuse. You can't. Fear won't let you. If you want to start being happy, you have to stop being afraid. What you're going through can either be a curse or a catalyst. The choice is yours.

#57 Don't Wear Skinny Jeans

MEN: If you look good in skinny jeans, you're too skinny. I understand you want to look like a rockstar. But unless you're Mick Jagger, sporting jeans tight enough to reveal veins is trying too hard. Look your age. Wear pants that fit.

WOMEN: Don't lie to him and say they look good. Be honest. Tell him he looks like a pigeon.

#58 Do Play with Your Legos

MEN: It doesn't matter if you're building a treehouse or an empire. Men are meant to build things. There is growth in the process of creating, carving, lining up parts to execute a vision. It gives you a sense of purpose and accomplishment. The result is a greater sense of self.

But remember, the value is not in what you have built or are building. It's in the struggle, sweat, failures, passion, persistence, courage, attitude, vision, dreams, and lessons that manifest from the act. That is the nectar of playing with your Legos. Not showing your friends what you have created.

WOMEN: Men who build know what it means to invest in something. They have callouses, not only on their hands but their determination. They are on a roller coaster instead of spinning tea cups. So ask yourself, before you decide which ride you want to get on. Do you prefer a rush or nausea?

#59 Don't Go For the Hottest Girl in the Room

MEN: If the person you are attracted to happens to be the hottest girl in the room, so be it. Great. But if you find yourself always pursuing the hottest girl in the room strictly because she is the hottest girl in the room, that means you want a trophy not a girlfriend. If you're looking for a badge or someone you believe will increase your worth, you are not confident with yourself which means you can not handle the hottest girl in the room. You will be clingy, jealous, controlling, and ultimately powerless. So don't waste all that time and energy and just go for who you are drawn to, not who you think we are. Because let's face it, there will always be someone "hotter". That means you will always feel incomplete.

WOMEN: You may feel honored if you date a man who's collection of ex-girlfriends lays out like the Swimsuit Edition of Sports Illustrated. But you do have to ask yourself two questions. One, what does that say about him? Two, and more importantly, what does that say about you?

#60 Don't Ogle Women

The difference between a look and a stare has less to do with duration and more to do with what's behind it. Behind a glance, there is curiosity and wonder. This leaves just enough room for appreciation and a compliment. Behind a stare, there is fantasy and possible intent. Cognition is happening. Thoughts are being processed. Energy is shifting.

MEN: If we are in a relationship, these thoughts will cause hairline cracks. For her, feeling undervalued and unappreciated which she may internalize as not being good enough. Yes, she notices when you do it no matter how subtle you think you are. For us, allowing ourselves to imagine what's behind the golden curtain. The more stares, the more you will fantasize about the prize or prizes, and the more cracks your relationship will have to endure. Enough of these cracks and the leg of trust falls. The table will tip. She will find someone who thinks *she's* the prize. Or you will hop that fence. Curiosity does not damage relationships. Fantasy and intent does.

If you drop more slips into the fantasy box instead of the appreciation box, you are getting on a roller coaster that does not stop. You will be dizzy and nauseous, living in a world of "what ifs" instead of "what is". Instead of investing, you are chasing. This means ultimately you will be very lonely.

The other piece. When we stare, we pass that line of appreciation and storm into personal space. Yes, you don't have to be physically near someone to enter their space. You can do it with your eyes. Ogling women is a respect thing. You are violating someone's personal space.

WOMEN: If your man says he doesn't look, he is either blind or lying. We are visual creatures. Aesthetics turn us on. It's how we are wired. Like little kids, we are fascinated by shapes, color, and design. But, there is a difference between a glance and a stare. If he has a habit of staring, ogling, invading other people's space, you not only have a right but an obligation to address this. If you do not, you are allowing him to drift and by allowing it you are not being responsible for your part in the relationship. Mention it once. If he doesn't change. Tell him how that makes you feel. If he still doesn't change, find someone who will.

#61 Do Express Your Feelings

Women are emotional. Men are logical. Okay, I get that. We've heard this a million times. But that doesn't change the fact that self expression is a fundamental piece of the relationship engine and without it, the relationship does not move forward or grow.

MEN / WOMEN: Expressing yourself is not a luxury. It is an obligation. By not disclosing how you feel, you are leaving the other person in the dark. This is irresponsible. If you can't do it for yourself, you must do it for the relationship because it's at stake. It's that plain and simple. Self expression is what holds relationships together. It's glue. Without it the relationship will fall apart. It's just a matter of time.

Self expression is like flossing. If you don't do it daily, you will have decay.

#62 Do Date Responsibly

I am not referring to being punctual, having manners, or using protection. Responsibility means asking yourself one question, *Are you ready?* Many jump into the dating process shorty after a break up and fall back into the same dysfunctional patterns. *Ready* means knowing why the last relationship did not work and your contribution to the expiration. It means to accept, explore, learn from, and decide to make a change so that the next one is healthier. Ready is not a completion. It is a process. It is a path. The question is are you on this path? If you are, you are being responsible. If you are not, you are contributing to spreading pain as well as stunting growth.

MEN / WOMEN: Examples of being an irresponsible dater include, dating solely to get laid, dating because you feel like you're supposed to instead of wanting to, dating due to your fear of being alone, dating someone because you can't say no or don't want to hurt their feelings.

#63 Don't Walk Away During a Fight

MEN: I am not referring to bar fights, obviously. This refers to the arguments you have with your girlfriend or wife. Unless you express needing some time to be alone because of your emotional state but promise to come back to it, there is absolutely no excuse to walk away from a fight. None. Zero. Ziltch. The moment you walk away, you are leaving the relationship. What she is hearing is, *I don't care about you. I don't want to work on us. I don't care how you feel. I cannot control my feelings. I'm done. I want out. Deal with it on your own. I don't love you.* Actions speak louder than words. Always. So if this is what you want to communicate, walk. But remember, she may not be there when you return. Or she may be there physically, but her heart will leave, slowly but surely.

It's not about how many times we fight. It's about how we fight. Fight fair. Use *I* statements. Understand before trying to be understood. And don't walk away.

WOMEN: If he leaves during conflict without providing a valid reason, either he doesn't have the tools to build you a safe container or he doesn't want to. Either way, he is preventing your growth which is something you should not be willing to negotiate. If you are, let him walk because you shouldn't be in this relationship.

64 Do Tell Your Children They are Good

Most of my clients are unaware of their value. They struggle with their worth. This contributes to the people they choose to surround themselves with and the kind of relationships they seek. What one believes they are worth starts with their parents. If their parents did not provide a safe, trusting and loving space demonstrating healthy support and love, the child will grow up with false beliefs about themselves. These false beliefs will allow them to negotiate themselves which will ultimately block their potential and cause a lot of pain.

FATHERS: Tell your daughter she is beautiful. Tell your son you are proud of him for who he is, not what he can do. Be the kind of man your daughter will use as a standard. Model the behavior by loving her mom, with respect, honor, and a big heaping spoonful of public affection. Know that they will see this as an example, a non-negotiable. Spend time with them. Make every moment count. Be genuinely interested in the things that interest them. Make them feel beautiful and invincible so that they know what to look for when they grow up. Know that what you say and how you treat them will directly affect the choices they will make later in life. Be the dad you never had, the one you've always wanted.

MOTHERS: The same goes for you: make sure your husband or boyfriend not only has the ability to do this but also chooses to do it daily. It should be important to him, something he chooses to define himself by. Your choice in men is not just about you.

#65 Do Have a Purpose

Imagine a tire. It is flat and spinning in mud. If you decide to become self aware and take your first step toward your inner journey, the tire begins to inflate. When you begin to execute change by incorporating your revelations into action, exploring thoughts and behavior, breaking unhealthy patterns, and walking in this new version of yourself, nobbies begin to appear on the tire. This traction causes movement. The tire is no longer spinning. You are moving.

Once you are out of the mud, sooner or later there will be more rough terrain. You may get stuck many more times. But if through your growth process you discover your purpose, those nobbies turn into giant titanium claws. No matter what terrain or mountain lies ahead, your knowing who you are and what you were meant to do will get you up, over, and through.

Knowing your purpose is the ultimate traction in life. It is a Sherman tank. You will be unstoppable. In order to know your purpose, you must do a self inventory, face your defects, review your story. You must confront, accept, and forgive. You must strip what has been processed and live in your truest form. Simply put, you must grow.

MEN: Every man must ask himself two questions. One, where is he going? And two, who's going with him? If he reverses the order, he will be going alone.

WOMEN: He doesn't have to know his purpose. For some, it's a life long process. He just has to have a dog-with-a-bone desire to seek it. The ride of your life not in his purpose. It's in his drive to seek one.

#66 Don't Whine

The ability to change one's attitude separates a boy from a man. Boys act out how they feel. They verbally vomit, hold grudges, and throw things. Simply put, they make it about them. Men are aware of their feelings but also how their words, behavior, and mood affect others. They have the ability to adjust, adapt, and control their behavior. They make it about others.

MEN: Whining can come in different forms. If you constantly complain about your life or work but do nothing about it, you're a whiner. If you pout when you don't get your way, from slamming doors to giving the silent treatment, you are a whiner. If you make someone go through what you're going through instead of expressing what you're going through, you are a whiner.

WOMEN: Men who whine were usually enabled as children. Most likely, they were the "baby", the youngest in sibling position. They are used to getting what they want and when they don't get it, they don't know how to cope with that anxiety. Therefore, whining or pouting just means he doesn't have tools.

So what do you do if you're in love with a whiner?
First, validate him. Validating his feelings will calm
him. It will defuse his desire to throw peas at the
wall. Once he is calm, you can speak to him like an
adult. Now tighten the vice and tell him how you feel
about his behavior and that it's not fair to you. Be
firm. Let him know how it affects your life, the
relationship, and your feelings toward him. That's it.
You've done your part. Now it's on him. He has a
choice to either start the process of growing up or to
lose you.

#67 Do Be Kind

Kind doesn't mean nice. There is a difference. Kind comes from heart. It is pure, without strings, and without condition. It is a genuine positive regard. Kind is gentle. Kind is a gift.

Nice can be a product of insecurity. Nice can be processed. Nice can be lined with fear. Nice can be approval seeking. Nice can be false. Nice can be taking. Nice can be forced. Nice can be a negotiation.

MEN: You know that saying, nice guys finish last? There is truth to it. They finish last because their focus to constantly please others causes them to lose their stance. Without their stance, it's impossible to find their truth. Woman want two things: trust and truth. Men can provide both. Boys can not. Be kind, not nice.

WOMEN: A nice man can practice empathy, forgiveness, and congruence, but a kind man can do it without sacrificing self.

#68 Do Believe in Yourself

MEN: You were meant to change the world. Your job is to find out how you're going to do it. There is no other way to look at life. If you don't, you will be a leaf. You will float around, get lost in your relationships, and be powerless. You will seek approval and validation, drown in false beliefs, and waste what you were blessed with.

Knowing your value, ability, and purpose is a process. For some it takes a lifetime, but you can not be on that journey until you first believe in yourself. That being said, there are going to be days you don't believe in yourself. There are going to be days when you feel like you were not meant to change anything. That is okay. That is part of the process. Believing in yourself is not a constant. It is a mindset and it takes times, effort, and work. It's less about the trudge and more about the choice to be on that path.

WOMEN: Men get discouraged. Men doubt themselves. Men make mistakes. It is important that you support, encourage and forgive, that you create a space for them to feel invincible so that they can make you feel beautiful.

Women, go find your perfect man.

That was a joke. There is no such thing. Perfect just means he realizes he's not.

Men, go change the world.

That was not a joke.

Man is nothing else but what he makes of himself.

- Jean Paul Sartre

ABOUT THE AUTHOR

John Kim is a licensed Marriage Family Therapist. In 2010, he started a blog called The Angry Therapist. Partly to document his own journey but also to create a dialogue that may help others. Coaching people online was not his intent but by the end of that year, he had two clients. By the end of the second year, he had coached over 100 people from all over the globe, treating individuals, couples, and facilitating groups. All from his computer. Due to the overwhelming response, he quit his 9 to 5 and opened a "public" practice. He defines his practice as "public" because he does everything online, including individual sessions, couples, and group work using Google Hangouts. Today, John uses his blog as a conduit to collect stories, create a dialgoue that may help others, and coach people from all over the world using the internet as a therapuetic tool.

You can meet him at -

www.theangrytherapist.com

More books from The Angry Therapist

"Self help in a shot glass". A self help book for people that don't like self help books. Less fat, more stick. John Kim's first book and introduction to his concepts through the telling of his personal story.

This journal is formatted so you can express yourself any way you wish. Write. Draw. Collage. Dialogue. Pie chart. Finger paint. Do what ever you feel. Just get it out.

A look into the mental and emotional side of CrossFit and how it affects performance. MindSet includes mental tips to improve your performance as well as a guide to explore, process, and dissolve your mental blocks.